A **TRUE** BOOK™

T0191338

THE EARTH AT RISK

DESERTS IN DANGER

Cody Crane

Children's Press®
An imprint of Scholastic Inc.

Content Consultants

Jenifer Utz, Ph.D. and Frank van Breukelen, Ph.D.

School of Life Sciences

University of Nevada, Las Vegas

Library of Congress Cataloging-in-Publication Data available

ISBN 978-1-5461-0218-2 (library binding) | ISBN 978-1-5461-0219-9 (paperback) | ISBN 978-1-5461-0220-5 (ebook)

10 9 8 7 6 5 4 3 2 1   25 26 27 28 29

Printed in China 62

First edition, 2025

Design by Kathleen Petelinsek

Series produced by Spooky Cheetah Press

Front cover: Today, the desert biome is facing several threats, such as over-development, mining, and wildfires.

Find the Truth!

Everything you are about to read is true *except* for one of the sentences on this page.

Which one is **TRUE**?

T or F   The largest desert on Earth is found in Antarctica.

T or F   Very few people live in deserts.

Find the answers in this book.

What's in This Book?

The Namib is a cool coastal desert that is found on the western coast of Africa.

The **BIG** Truth

Deathstalker scorpions are most often found in the deserts of Northern Africa and the Middle East. They are very dangerous!

Deserts Are Spreading

3 Deserts Under Threat

Saguaro cactuses are found in the Sonoran Desert in the United States and Mexico.

INTRODUCTION

A **desert** is any region that gets no more than 10 inches (25 centimeters) of **precipitation** a year. That makes deserts the world's driest **biome**. Some deserts are **scorching hot**. Others are **freezing cold**. Despite these harsh conditions, many plants and animals live in deserts. But their **homes are under threat**. Human activities have put deserts across the planet in danger. Luckily, people are **working to help save** these wild places.

Rainforests get about 10 times more precipitation than deserts.

Black-maned lions live in the Kalahari Desert in Africa.

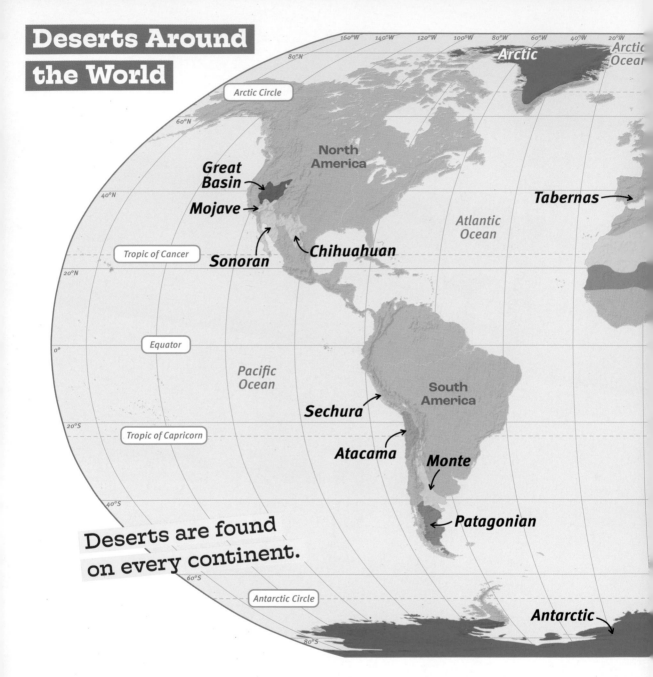

Deserts are found on every continent.

The desert biome can be broken down into **four main ecosystems**: hot and dry, semiarid, cold, and coastal.

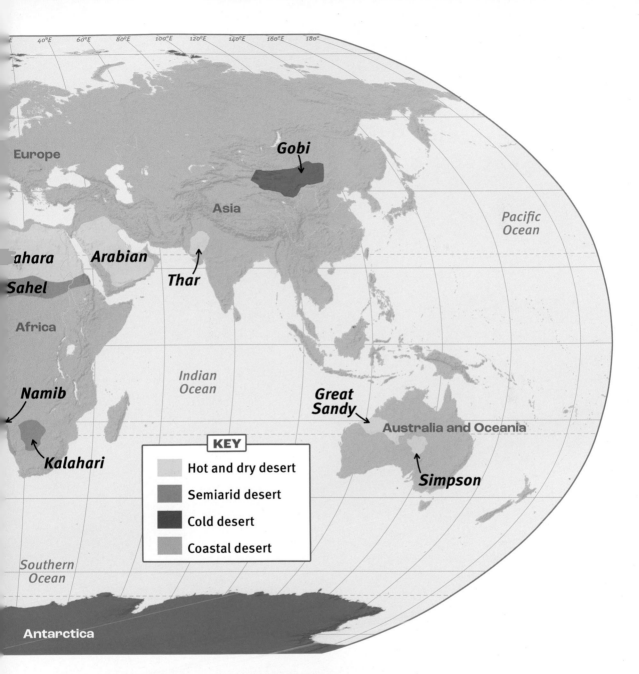

Map labels:
40°E 60°E 80°E 100°E 120°E 140°E 160°E 180°

Europe

Gobi

Asia

Pacific
Ocean

ahara   Arabian

Sahel   Thar

Africa

Indian
Ocean

Namib   Great
Sandy

Australia and Oceania

Kalahari   KEY

Hot and dry desert

Semiarid desert   Simpson

Cold desert

Coastal desert

Southern
Ocean

Antarctica

This map shows where **deserts** are located around the world. It also includes the names of some of the largest and best-known deserts.

In Arabic, the word ṣaḥrā means "desert."

The Sahara is the largest hot and dry desert. Sand covers about 25 percent of its area.

Hot Shots

PHEW! Things can really heat up in hot and dry and semiarid deserts. Hot and dry deserts are the more extreme of the two. Daytime temperatures there can reach 100 degrees Fahrenheit (38 degrees Celsius) or more year-round. Precipitation in these deserts varies depending on location. Parts of the Mojave Desert in the United States can get 8.5 in. (21.6 cm) of rain a year. Areas of the Sahara in Africa get just 1 in. (2.5 cm).

The Sentinel Mesa is located in Monument Valley, which is on the border of Utah and Arizona in the United States.

Rocks and Sand

Hot and dry deserts have flat, rocky areas as well as rolling sand dunes. Rain and wind can wear down rocks over thousands of years. This creates unusual landforms like tall, flat-topped hills called mesas. Wind often blows the desert's loose sandy soil into piles, forming dunes.

Duna Federico Kirbus in Argentina is the world's tallest sand dune. It is about 4,035 feet (1,230 meters) tall.

Water in the Desert

It does not rain much in hot and dry deserts. But it is still possible to find water there. There are rivers in this type of desert. We can also find oases. These are places in the desert where underground water rises to the surface.

The water may come from a natural spring or a well that was dug by people. Many plants and trees grow around an oasis because there is plenty of water. Animals visit the oasis to find water, food, and shade.

An oasis has very fertile ground. Crops such as cotton, dates, olives, and figs can be grown there.

People traveling through the desert may use an oasis as a resting spot.

Rain Catchers

Only a few plants dot the landscape in most areas of hot and dry deserts. Many have adaptations to survive in dry conditions. Creosote bushes and fountain grass have widespread roots. They quickly soak up as much water as possible when it rains. Many plants, like agave, have leaves that overlap around their centers to funnel rainwater toward their roots.

creosote bush

fountain grass

agave

Some hot and dry desert plants have one long root that can reach water hundreds of feet underground.

Water Savers

Succulents are desert plants that have thick, fleshy tissues to store water. Some, like cactuses, save up water in their stems. Some cactus stems even have folds that allow them to expand when they absorb rainwater. Other succulents store water in their thick, waxy leaves. Yucca plants are succulents that store water in their roots.

Saguaro cactuses can live up to 200 years!

yucca

saguaro

Some cactuses have sharp needles. Needles help protect the plant's stored water from thirsty animals.

Cool Behavior

Animals in hot and dry deserts have also adapted to the climate. Desert tortoises and kangaroo rats rest in the shade or underground during the day. Some animals like sidewinder rattlesnakes are active at dawn and dusk. Deathstalker scorpions are nocturnal. They hunt at night when the temperature is cooler. Many creatures get most of the water they need from the food they eat.

desert tortoise

kangaroo rat

sidewinder rattlesnake

deathstalker scorpion

camel

fennec fox

jackrabbit

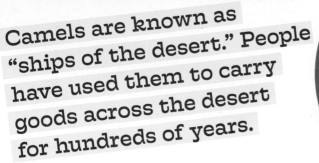
Camels are known as "ships of the desert." People have used them to carry goods across the desert for hundreds of years.

Helpful Features

Many of the animals here also have physical adaptations that help them survive. Camels can close their nostrils. They also have long eyelashes. That keeps sand out of their nose and eyes. Fennec foxes and jackrabbits have large ears that draw heat away from their bodies.

The Sahel is a semiarid region in Africa that borders the Sahara.

Semiarid deserts are often found on the edges of hot and dry deserts.

Not-So-Hot

Semiarid deserts are not as hot or dry as hot and dry deserts. Temperatures in semiarid deserts usually do not rise above 100°F (38°C). And more rain can fall in these areas than in hot and dry deserts. Semiarid deserts are rocky and flat and may have dunes. A few lakes and rivers provide water for people and wildlife.

Greener Landscape

Semiarid deserts have more plants than hot and dry deserts do. The ground may be covered in grasses and shrubs, like sage. These plants often have pale, fuzzy, or glossy leaves that reflect sunlight. This keeps the plants cool. Semiarid deserts can also have hardy trees, like baobabs, junipers, eucalyptus, and palms.

sage

Baobab trees are found in semiarid parts of Africa. They have spongy bark to soak up water.

juniper

eucalyptus

Plant-Eaters

Because semiarid deserts have a variety of plants, a wide range of **herbivores** can live there. Jerboas and cockatoos are small plant-eaters that will sometimes eat insects too. Large herbivores include guanacos, elephants, and bighorn sheep. All these big animals travel in herds to find sources of water.

jerboa

cockatoo

guanaco

Elephants are the largest animals that live in the desert.

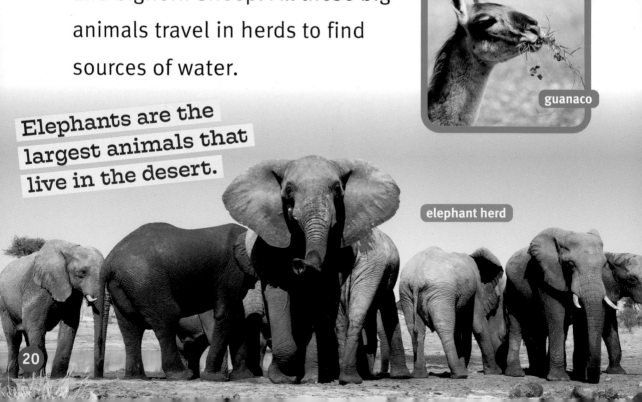

elephant herd

Desert Hunters

Semiarid deserts support a lot of meat-eaters too. In Africa, those include cheetahs, mongoose, and hyenas. In North America, there are coyotes, snakes, and mountain lions. The Sechuran fox lives in South America, and the marbled polecat can be found in Asia. These animals often have brown fur to blend into their surroundings.

Vultures are desert scavengers. These large birds of prey feed on dead animals they find.

cheetah

coyote

Sechuran fox

marbled polecat

Emperor penguins live in Antarctica—which is also where the world's largest desert is found.

The ice covering Antarctica is about 1.2 miles (2 kilometers) thick!

CHAPTER 2

Cool Customers

The Arctic and Antarctic Deserts are two examples of cold deserts. Average temperatures there rarely rise above freezing, or 32°F (0°C). What little precipitation they receive falls as snow instead of rain. Each year 5 to 10 in. (13 to 25 cm) of snow falls in the Arctic Desert. The interior of the Antarctic gets just 2 in. (5 cm). Ice covers both deserts year-round.

Polar Living

It is too cold for most plants to survive in deserts close to the North and South Poles. In many areas, only lichen and mosses grow. Few animals can survive either. Seals and penguins in Antarctica have a layer of fat to keep them warm. In the Arctic, polar bears, Arctic hares, and Arctic foxes have fur to keep warm.

seals

Polar bears are the world's largest predators found on land.

polar bear

Arctic hare

Arctic fox

Mountain Deserts

Cold deserts also exist in high-**altitude** regions in mountain ranges. However, these deserts are cold only for part of the year. Temperatures can vary a lot. For example, the Gobi is a cold mountain desert in Asia. Temperatures range from −40°F (−40°C) in cold months to 113°F (45°C) in warm months!

winter

summer

The Gobi Desert covers an area three times the size of Sweden.

25

Life in the Heights

Cold mountain deserts are rocky and have dunes. The land is covered with shrubs and grasses. In the Gobi, these plants provide food for wild donkeys, Bactrian camels, and small rodents. There are also snow leopards and golden eagles there. In the Great Basin Desert in the United States, animals include elk, mountain lions, pack rats, and bats.

The Gobi Desert is one of the few places where wild camels are found. Most camels are raised by people.

wild donkey

snow leopard

golden eagle

elk

Coastal Deserts

Coastal deserts have mild, cool temperatures year-round and almost no rain. They form next to the ocean where there are cold ocean currents offshore. The moving water cools the air above the ocean. That causes rain to fall on the ocean instead of the land. Fog from the ocean often covers coastal deserts. But heat from the sun causes water in the fog to **evaporate** before it can become rain.

The Atacama Desert in South America is used as a training ground for missions to Mars.

Atacama Desert

The Namib Desert in Africa is a coastal desert. It is considered the oldest desert on Earth.

Deserts Are

Each year, about 46,000 square mi. (120,000 sq. km) of land becomes new desert. That is an area almost four times the size of the state of Maryland. That is because of desertification.

1

Loss of Plants

The following activities remove plants from the soil or make it so plants can no longer grow.

- Farming uses up all the nutrients in the soil.
- Grazing animals, like cattle and sheep, strip an area of its plants.
- People cut down forests.
- People use up an area's water.

Spreading

Desertification happens when human activities damage lands around deserts, causing them to turn into desert. It also destroys the natural homes of plants and wildlife. Here is how it happens.

This conceptual image shows the process of desertification.

2 Soil Disappears

The roots of plants help keep soil in place. Without them, wind and rain carry soil away.

3 Desert Spreads

Without soil, the ground becomes rocky and bare. Few new plants can grow. The area becomes a desert.

During the winter of 2019–2020, extreme desert wildfires in Australia killed more than one billion animals.

Drier conditions caused by climate change can lead to intense wildfires in deserts.

Deserts Under Threat

Deserts may seem like hardy places, but they still face many threats. One of the biggest is **climate change**. It is making deserts hotter and drier. Mining, farming, and cities built in deserts are problems too. All these activities damage and change the natural landscape. As a result, some of the animals that live in deserts are **endangered**. More people, like you, are learning about these issues. They are finding ways to help protect desert ecosystems.

Heating Up

Climate change is causing warmer temperatures. As a result, ice covering land in the Arctic and Antarctic Deserts is melting. This contributes to rising sea levels around the world, endangering coastal habitats and the people who live there. Warmer temperatures also make desert wildfires more likely. All these changes make it harder for desert wildlife to survive.

Timeline: Deserts Under Stress

1920
Recordkeeping on the size of the Sahara begins. It has expanded by 10 percent since this date.

1950s
The Gobi, the fastest-growing desert on Earth, begins to spread.

1978
The Great Green Wall project begins to plant a forest to stop the advance of the Gobi Desert.

Desert Invaders

Farmers often allow animals to graze in deserts. Livestock eat desert plants, leaving areas totally bare. People have also introduced **invasive species**—accidentally and on purpose. Invasive weeds can choke out native, or local, desert plants. Invasive animals can eat native plants and wildlife. Eventually, the invaders take over.

1992
Due to climate change, Antarctica and Greenland have lost about 6.4 trillion tons of ice since this date.

2020
Wildfire destroys about one million Joshua trees in the Mojave Desert.

2050
Scientists predict that about one-fourth of the land on Earth will be deserts—up from one-fifth in 2023.

Digging up the Desert

Deserts contain many natural resources, including minerals, metals, and fossil fuels like oil and coal. These resources are needed to build and power most modern technology. Most have to be dug or drilled out of the ground, which destroys large areas of desert ecosystems. Mining also creates pollution that can harm desert plants and animals.

Nuclear waste from power plants is often buried in deserts. This waste is extremely dangerous to living things.

Fossil fuels are found beneath the ice in the Arctic Desert.

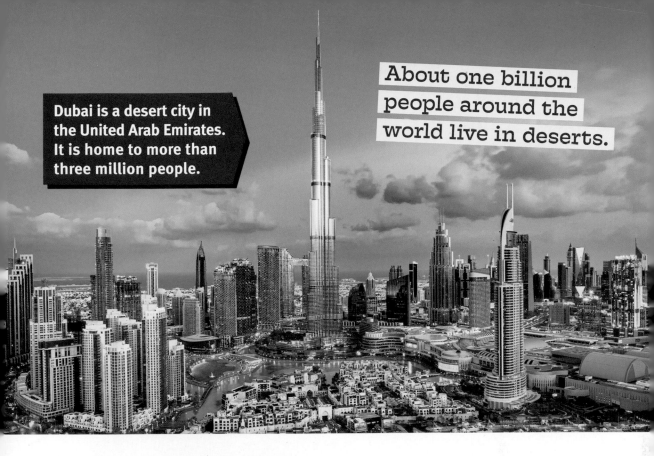

Dubai is a desert city in the United Arab Emirates. It is home to more than three million people.

About one billion people around the world live in deserts.

Expanding Cities

Many large cities lie in deserts. They take over more of the landscape as they grow. People in desert cities need lots of water. They get it by building dams on nearby rivers or tapping into underground sources. This water is also used to grow crops. That leaves less water and land for desert plants and animals.

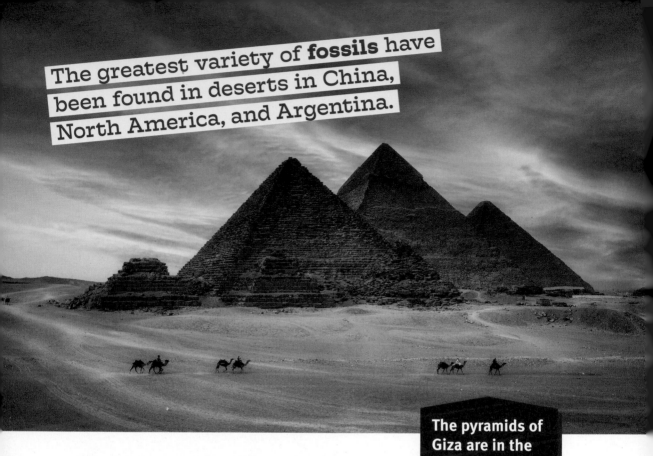

The greatest variety of **fossils** have been found in deserts in China, North America, and Argentina.

The pyramids of Giza are in the Sahara.

Preserving the Past

A desert's dry climate is perfect for preserving things. That is why most fossils are found there. Important archaeological sites are found in the desert too. These sites include prehistoric rock drawings and Egyptian pyramids. All of these teach us about the past. Threats to deserts put what we can learn about the past in danger.

Desert Peoples

Indigenous peoples have lived in deserts for thousands of years. Some desert-dwellers continue to live a traditional way of life like their ancestors. They know how to survive in desert ecosystems without harming them. For example, Bedouins who live in the Arabian Desert move from place to place. They travel to find water and allow their herds of sheep, goats, or camels to graze. Others, like the Inuit people who live in the Arctic, fish, hunt, and gather native wild plants as part of their traditional diets.

An Inuit fisherman in Greenland

A Bedouin camp in Jordan

A Helping Hand

Deserts are at risk around the world. But people are finding ways to help them. Some restore and protect native plants and wildlife. Others remove invasive species. Thanks to the work of conservationists, new mining and drilling projects must show they will not harm the ecosystem before they will be approved. Desert cities are using land and water more wisely. And people everywhere are working to fight climate change.

Volunteers remove invasive plants in Saguaro National Park in Arizona.

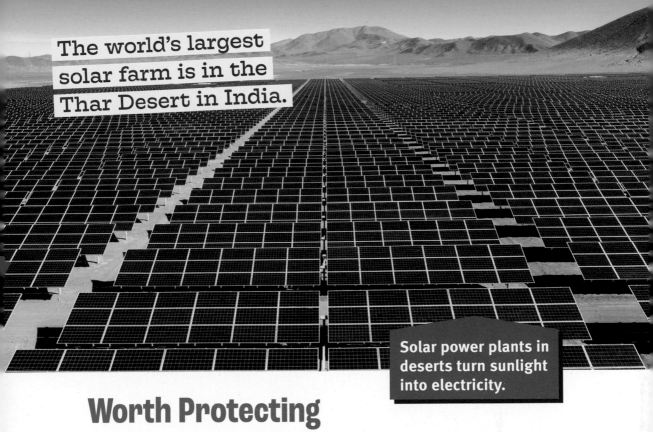

The world's largest solar farm is in the Thar Desert in India.

Solar power plants in deserts turn sunlight into electricity.

Worth Protecting

Now you know that deserts are not bare, lifeless places. In fact, they are home to plants and animals found nowhere else on Earth. Deserts are home to people too. And they hold important resources and history. Changes to deserts, like melting ice at the poles, can have an impact on the entire planet. All these are reasons why we should protect this amazing biome!

Amazing Comeback

Meet the Arabian oryx (OR-icks)—an antelope that is perfectly suited for life in the desert. The oryx's wide hooves help it walk over sand. Its white fur reflects heat from the sun to keep it cool. And it can survive by drinking very little water.

The oryx once roamed across the Arabian Desert. But people hunted the animal for its meat and horns. By the 1960s, few oryx were left in the wild. So a group that works to protect wild animals formed a plan. It was called "Operation Oryx."

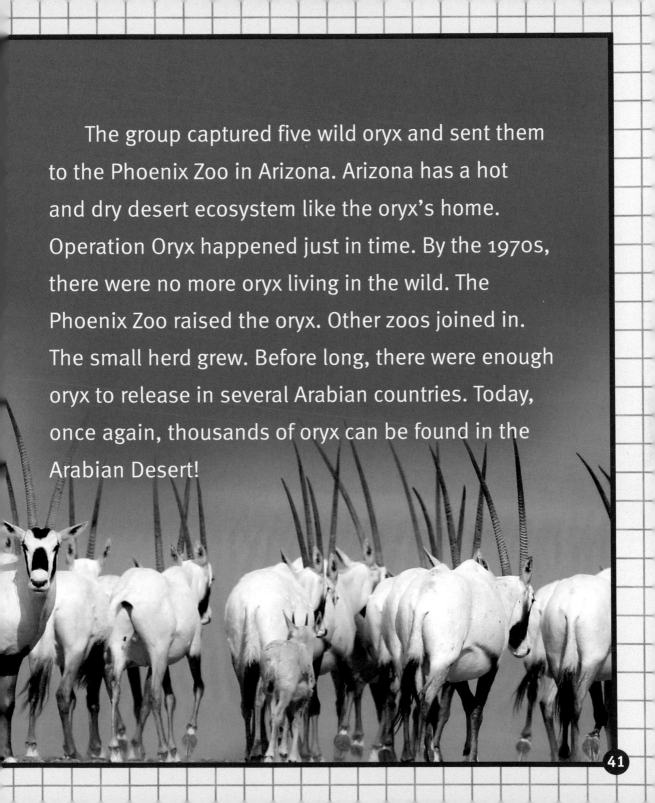

The group captured five wild oryx and sent them to the Phoenix Zoo in Arizona. Arizona has a hot and dry desert ecosystem like the oryx's home. Operation Oryx happened just in time. By the 1970s, there were no more oryx living in the wild. The Phoenix Zoo raised the oryx. Other zoos joined in. The small herd grew. Before long, there were enough oryx to release in several Arabian countries. Today, once again, thousands of oryx can be found in the Arabian Desert!

Kid Heroes

Charlotte (12), Tallis (10), and Serenity Icely (8) are working to help protect the desert near their home in Tucson, Arizona. The girls and their mom, Brittany, are members of the Sonoran Desert Weedwackers. These volunteers work to remove an invasive weed called buffelgrass from this hot and dry desert. Here, the Icely sisters answer some questions about their work.

Brittany

1

Q: What is buffelgrass?

A: It is an invasive plant. It normally grows in Africa, the Middle East, and Asia. Decades ago, it was planted in dry parts of the United States as a food for cattle. People did not realize at the time that buffelgrass would spread everywhere!

2

Q: Why is buffelgrass a threat to the ecosystem?

A: It takes over, so there is no room for native plants. And if buffelgrass catches fire, it burns very hot. It can cause more intense wildfires. That puts the desert at risk. It also puts the homes and lives of people who live nearby at risk.

Charlotte

Tallis

buffelgrass

Serenity

3

Q: **How do you and the other Weedwackers help?**

A: We meet up and hike into the desert to remove buffelgrass. We have tools that look a bit like poles. We use them to pry the weeds out of the ground. We spend about four hours each trip.

4

Q: **What do you like about being a Weedwacker?**

A: It is nice to see all the native desert plants and animals and know that you are helping them. We are usually the only kid volunteers. It is a lot of hard work. But you feel really accomplished afterward. It makes you realize kids can make a difference and help heal the landscape!

True Statistics *

Height of the tallest saguaro cactus in the world: 78 feet (24 m)—found in the Sonoran Desert, United States

Number of domesticated camels in the world: 35 million

Number of wild camels in the world: 950

Hottest temperature ever recorded on Earth: 134°F (57°C)—in Death Valley in California's Mojave Desert

Coldest temperature ever recorded on Earth: –128.6°F (–89.2°C)—Antarctic Desert

Size of the biggest desert on Earth: 5.5 million square miles (14.2 million sq. km)— Antarctic Desert

* As of 2024

Did you find the truth?

T The largest desert on Earth is found in Antarctica.

F Very few people live in deserts.

Resources

Other books in this series:

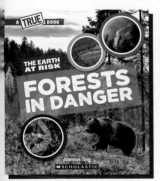
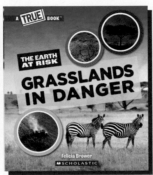
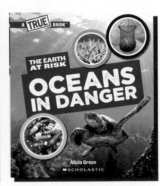

You can also look at:

Bash, Barbara. *Desert Giant: The World of the Saguaro Cactus*. San Francisco: Sierra Club Books for Children, 2002.

Fabiny, Sarah. *Where Is the Sahara Desert?* New York: Penguin Workshop, 2023.

Gibbons, Gail. *Deserts*. New York: Holiday House, 1999.

Glossary

altitude (AL-ti-tood) the height of something above the ground or above sea level

biome (BYE-ohm) a region of the world with similar animals and plants

climate change (KLYE-mit CHAYNJ) global warming and other changes in the weather and weather patterns that are happening because of human activity

ecosystems (EE-koh-sis-tuhmz) all the living things in a place and their relation to their environment

endangered (en-DAYN-jurd) in danger of becoming extinct, usually because of human activity

evaporate (i-VAP-uh-rate) to change into a vapor or gas

fossils (FAH-suhlz) bones, shells, or other traces of an animal or a plant from millions of years ago, preserved as rock

herbivores (HUR-buh-vorz) animals that eat only plants

Indigenous peoples (in-DI-juh-nuhs PEE-puhlz) the first known inhabitants of a place

invasive species (in-VAY-siv SPEE-sheez) a plant, an insect, or an animal that is introduced to an area where it would not naturally occur

precipitation (pri-sip-i-TAY-shuhn) water that falls from the sky in the form of rain, sleet, hail, or snow